AF875437

The Etsy Listing That Earns Its Keep

A Calm, Practical Framework for Building Etsy Listings That Actually Work

Tracey Power Hilborn

The Curiosity Cabinet Press
United States of America

The Etsy Listing That Earns Its Keep:
A Calm, Practical Framework for Building Etsy Listings That Actually Work
Copyright © 2026 by Tracey Power Hilborn
All rights reserved.

No part of this book may be reproduced, stored, or transmitted by any means—electronic, mechanical, photocopying, recording, or otherwise—without written permission from the publisher, except for brief quotations used in reviews, critical articles, or educational contexts.

Published in the United States by:
The Curiosity Cabinet Press
www.thecuriositycabinetpress.com

ISBN: 978-1-967930-04-3

Our books may be purchased in bulk for educational, promotional, or business use.
For ordering inquiries, please contact:
orders@thecuriositycabinetpress.com

Printed in the United States of America
(The printer and distributor may vary by region.)

Table of Contents

This page intentionally left blank

Introduction

Why This Book Exists

If you've ever stared at one of your Etsy listings and thought,
"I don't know what else to fix,"
this book is for you.

Not because you haven't tried hard enough.
Not because you don't care.
And not because you "just don't get Etsy."

Most sellers who end up here are doing too much — not too little.

They've followed the advice.
They've changed titles.
They've swapped keywords.
They've rebuilt photos.
They've watched the videos, joined the groups, downloaded the checklists.

And somehow… things feel worse, not better.

This book was created to stop that spiral.

This Is Not Another Etsy "How-To"

You will not find:

- keyword hacks
- trend chasing
- daily optimization routines
- promises of fast growth
- pressure to fix everything at once

That kind of advice doesn't fail because sellers are lazy or incapable.
It fails because it ignores how real people actually buy — and how real sellers actually work.

This book was built from inside a real shop, using a real listing, with real data, real decline, and real recovery.

It exists to help you make **one good decision at a time**.

What This Book Will Help You Do

This guide will help you:

- decide which listings deserve your energy
- stop rebuilding listings that can't be saved
- understand what buyers need *before* they click "Add to Cart"
- create listings that feel calm, clear, and trustworthy
- let your work speak for itself without constant tweaking

Most importantly, it will help you stop treating your shop like a never-ending to-do list — and start treating it like a small system that can support you.

How to Use This Book

This is not a book you rush through.

You'll move section by section, working with:

- reflection prompts
- decision checkpoints
- simple worksheets
- honest evaluation

You don't need to complete everything in one sitting.
You don't need to fix your entire shop.
You only need **one listing** to begin.

Take your time.
Write in the margins.
Skip around if you need to.

This book is meant to sit beside you while you work — not talk at you from a distance.

One Last Thing Before You Begin

You are not behind because you failed.

You're behind because the rules changed, the advice multiplied, and no one ever showed you how to slow down and think clearly again.

That's what this book is here to do.

Let's begin.

SECTION 1

Does This Listing Deserve to Earn?

Before we talk about titles, photos, keywords, or Etsy's ever-changing advice, we have to start here — because this step alone will save you hours of wasted effort and years of frustration.

Not every listing deserves to be "fixed."

That's a hard truth, and it's one most Etsy advice skips right over. Instead, sellers are told to optimize everything: rewrite all the titles, redo all the photos, update all the tags, and just keep pushing harder.

But here's the reality:

Some listings don't need optimization.
They need honesty.

This guide is not about rescuing every idea you've ever had. It's about identifying the listings that should be earning — the ones that already have proof of life — and giving **those** your time and attention.

The Difference Between a Bad Listing and a Bad Offer

This matters more than anything else in this guide.

A **bad listing** is something good that's being explained poorly.
A **bad offer** is something people don't actually want — no matter how well you explain it.

Most sellers confuse the two.

If you try to "optimize" a bad offer, you will exhaust yourself and still see no results. That's not because you're doing it wrong — it's because you're working on the wrong thing.

So before we touch a single word or image, we ask one simple question:

> *Is this listing already trying to earn — or am I trying to force it?*

The Earnings Potential Reality Check

Answer these questions honestly. There is no prize for optimism here — clarity is the goal.

1. Has this listing ever sold?
Not "did someone favorite it." Not "did my cousin buy one."
Has a real, paying customer chosen this item?

One sale is not enough proof — but it is a signal.

2. Has it sold more than once?
Repeat sales mean the offer itself works.
If people have purchased it multiple times, the problem is rarely the product.

3. Do people ask questions about it?
Messages are friction — but they're also interest.
Questions mean buyers are close but uncertain.

4. Do people favorite it?
Favorites without sales usually indicate hesitation, not rejection.
That's important — hesitation can be fixed.

5. Is the problem traffic or conversion?
If people are seeing the listing but not buying, that's a clarity issue — not a demand issue.

6. Can a stranger understand what this is in five seconds?
If someone has to read carefully, zoom in, or "figure it out," the listing is doing too much work.

If you answered "yes" to even two or three of these questions, the listing is worth saving.

A Real Example (Why This Guide Exists)

One of the listings used in this guide — a DIY wood quilt block kit — had sold over a thousand units in earlier years. It had strong reviews, repeat buyers, and a proven audience.

And yet… sales had slowly declined.

Not because people stopped wanting it.
Not because the price was wrong.
Not because shipping was too high.

It declined because the listing stopped keeping up with how buyers think now.

The offer was still good.
The listing was tired.

That distinction changes everything.

Why This Step Comes First

If you skip this step, you'll do what most sellers do:

- Rewrite listings that never sold
- Spend hours fixing ideas the market already rejected
- Blame Etsy, the algorithm, or yourself

This guide is about doing less — better.

When you choose listings that deserve to earn, your work finally starts paying you back.

Pause Here (This Matters)

Before you move on:

- Pick one listing you believe should be earning
- Don't pick your newest idea
- Don't pick your favorite idea
- Pick the one with proof, even if it's old proof

That's the listing we'll work on next.

Because the goal isn't to make everything sell.

The goal is to make the right things earn their keep.

WORKBOOK PAGE — SECTION 1

Does This Listing Deserve to Earn?

Purpose:
Help the reader choose the right listing before doing any work.

> *You are not fixing everything.*
> *You are choosing wisely.*

Step 1: Choose One Listing

Write the name or URL of the listing you want to work on:

Step 2: Earnings Potential Reality Check

Answer honestly. No fixing yet.

Check all that apply:

- ☐ This listing has sold at least once
- ☐ It has sold more than once
- ☐ It has received favorites
- ☐ Buyers have messaged with questions
- ☐ It feels like it should be selling
- ☐ The product itself is solid
- ☐ The problem feels like clarity, not demand

If you checked 2 or more, this listing deserves your attention.

Step 3: Quick Gut Check

Finish this sentence:

> *"If this listing were clearer, I believe it could earn because…"*

SECTION 2

Stop Building Listings. Start Building Decisions.

Most Etsy sellers think they are building listings.

They are not.

They are building explanations.

And explanations don't sell.

Buyers don't come to Etsy to learn.
They don't come to research.
They don't come to understand your process, your story, or your effort.

They come to decide.

And if your listing doesn't help them decide — clearly, calmly, and quickly — they leave.

Not because they didn't like your product.
Because their brain got tired.

The Biggest Lie Sellers Are Taught

Here's the lie most of us were taught (directly or indirectly):

> *"If I just explain it better, people will buy."*

So we:

- add more words
- add more photos
- add more keywords
- add more detail
- add more sections

And somehow… sales still don't happen.

Because **clarity is not the same thing as information.**

You can explain something perfectly and still fail to sell it.

How Buyers Actually Move Through a Listing

This is the part no one explains — and once you see it, you can't unsee it.

Buyers do **not** move through a listing in order.

They:

- glance at the first image
- skim the title
- swipe images quickly
- scroll halfway down
- bounce back up
- look for something that makes them feel safe

They are asking silent questions the entire time.

Not out loud.
Not logically.
Emotionally.

Questions like:

- "Is this for someone like me?"
- "Am I going to mess this up?"
- "Is this more work than I think?"
- "Will I regret buying this?"
- "Why haven't I seen this before?"
- "Is this worth the money?"

If your listing doesn't answer those questions before they fully form, the buyer leaves — even if they liked the product.

Listings Are Decision Tools, Not Product Descriptions

This is the mental shift that changes everything.

A good listing does not describe a product.

A good listing **removes reasons not to buy.**

Think about that.

You are not convincing someone to want your item.
You are helping someone who already wants it feel safe enough to say yes.

That's why:

- more keywords don't help
- longer descriptions don't help
- "perfect" photos don't help

What helps is **intentional structure.**

Why More Is Often Worse

When sellers feel stuck, they usually add.

But adding does this:

- increases cognitive load
- creates new questions
- introduces doubt
- makes buyers feel like they need to "figure it out"

Confused buyers don't buy.

Tired buyers don't buy.

Buyers who feel like they're missing something don't buy.

The Real Job of a Listing

Your listing has one job:

> **Guide a stranger from interest to confidence.**

That's it.

Not admiration.
Not education.
Not explanation.

Confidence.

When buyers feel confident, they don't hesitate.
When they don't hesitate, they buy.

What This Means for Everything That Comes Next

From this point forward in the guide:

- titles exist to orient
- images exist to reassure
- descriptions exist to steady
- FAQs exist to remove friction

Every piece has a job.
Nothing is accidental.
Nothing is filler.

We stop asking:

> *"What should I add?"*

And start asking:

> *"What decision am I helping them make right now?"*

That question alone will change how you build every listing from here on out.

Pause Here (Yes, Again)

Before moving on, I want you, the reader, to do this:

- Pull up one listing you believe should be earning
- Look at it and ask:
    - "What decision is this helping someone make?"
    - "Where does it feel shaky?"
    - "Where would I hesitate if I didn't already know this product?"

You don't fix anything yet.

You just notice.

Because once you see listings as decision tools instead of product pages, you can't go back.

And now — finally — we're ready to build something that earns its keep.

WORKBOOK PAGE — SECTION 2

Stop Building Listings. Start Building Decisions.

Purpose:
Shift from explaining to supporting buyer confidence.

Step 1: Silent Buyer Questions

Imagine a buyer scrolling quietly.
Write the questions they are asking *without typing them:*

1.

2.

3.

4.

(These are fears, not technical questions.)

Step 2: Where Does My Listing Ask Too Much?

Circle any that feel true:

My buyer has to figure things out
Important details are buried
I assume they understand my process
I explain instead of reassuring
The listing feels busy or heavy

Step 3: One Big Shift

Write one sentence:

"This listing would sell better if buyers felt more confident about…"

SECTION 3

The 5-Part Listing That Earns Its Keep

Once you understand that listings are decision tools, not product descriptions, the question becomes simple:

What decisions does a buyer need help making — and in what order?

Every listing that earns consistently does five things well.
Not ten. Not twenty. Five.

Miss one, and the listing leaks sales.
Get all five right, and even "old" listings can come back to life.

This is the framework we used to rebuild the quilt block listing — and the same framework you can apply to any listing that deserves to earn.

PART 1: Instant Recognition

"What is this — and is it for me?"

This decision happens in **seconds**.

If a buyer can't answer those two questions almost immediately, they don't keep reading — no matter how good the product is.

This is where:

- the title
- the hero image
- the overall vibe

must work together.

Not to impress — to orient.

The buyer should know:

- what category this belongs in
- what kind of experience it offers
- whether it fits their identity (beginner, experienced, gift buyer, etc.)

PART 2: Safety & Reassurance

"Can I do this without messing it up?"

This is the biggest silent stopper for DIY, handmade, and creative products.

Buyers are quietly asking:

- "Am I skilled enough?"
- "Is this harder than it looks?"
- "Will I regret buying this?"

They don't want to feel foolish.
They don't want to waste money.
They don't want a project that ends up unfinished.

This is where you:

- normalize fear
- lower the bar
- give permission

Clear steps.
Simple language.
Calm tone.

When buyers feel safe, they keep going.

PART 3: Effort Reality Check

"Is this more work than I'm imagining?"

This decision is about **time and energy**, not ability.

Buyers want to know:

- How long will this actually take?
- Is this a whole-day project or an evening one?

Will it take over my life or fit into it?

Ambiguity here causes hesitation.

Clear expectations reduce risk:

- "A couple of relaxed hours"
- "Finishable"
- "No special tools"

When buyers understand the effort, they stop imagining worst-case scenarios.

PART 4: Emotional Payoff

"Why will I be glad I bought this?"

This is where the listing stops being practical and becomes personal.

Buyers don't just buy objects — they buy:

- experiences
- feelings
- moments
- pride
- relief
- enjoyment

This is where you help them imagine:

- the process
- the satisfaction
- the finished result
- the reaction of others

Not in a hypey way — in a real way.

When buyers can picture themselves enjoying the outcome, buying feels natural.

PART 5: Decision Removal

"Answer what I'm afraid to ask."

This is where many listings fall apart.

Buyers hesitate because of small unanswered questions:

- "What size is it?"
- "What's actually included?"
- "Do I need special supplies?"
- "What if I buy it as a gift?"
- "What if something goes wrong?"

FAQs, clear images, and calm explanations remove these final barriers.

By the time a buyer reaches this point, they're not looking for excitement — they're looking for reassurance.

When nothing feels risky, the decision becomes easy.

Why This Framework Works

This structure:

- matches how buyers think
- respects how they browse
- reduces mental effort
- replaces hesitation with confidence

And most importantly:

It works **regardless of niche.**

You can sell:

- DIY kits
- printables
- handmade goods
- digital products
- vintage items

If your listing helps buyers move through these five decisions, it earns.

How to Use This Framework

You do **not** rewrite everything at once.

You:

1. Identify which part your listing is weak in
2. Fix that part only
3. Let the listing settle
4. Observe what changes

Most sellers fail because they try to fix everything at the same time.

This system prevents that.

Pause Here (Again — on purpose)

Before moving on:

- Look at your chosen listing
- Ask yourself:
    - Which of these five parts is weakest?
    - Where would a buyer hesitate?
    - Where does the listing ask too much of them?

You don't change anything yet.

You're learning to see listings differently.

And once you see them this way, you never go back.

WORKBOOK PAGE — SECTION 3

The 5-Part Listing Checkup

Purpose:
Identify which part of the listing is leaking sales.

Step 1: Choose ONE Area to Fix

Rate Each Section (1 = weak, 5 = strong)

1. Instant Recognition
What is this, and is it for me?

1☐ 2☐ 3☐ 4☐ 5☐

2. Safety & Reassurance
Can I do this without messing up?

1☐ 2☐ 3☐ 4☐ 5☐

3. Effort Reality Check
Is this manageable in real life?

1☐ 2☐ 3☐ 4☐ 5☐

4. Emotional Payoff
Why will I be glad I bought this?

1☐ 2☐ 3☐ 4☐ 5☐

5. Decision Removal
Are my last questions answered?

1☐ 2☐ 3☐ 4☐ 5☐

Step 2: Choose ONE Area to Fix

The weakest area above is:

That is the only thing you will focus on first.

SECTION 4

The Quilt Block Listing - Before & After

Everything in this guide exists because of one real listing.

Not a mockup.
Not a hypothetical.
Not a cherry-picked success story.

A listing that:

- had sold well in the past
- slowly declined over time
- still had a good product behind it
- but had stopped earning its keep

This is the listing we rebuilt — deliberately, calmly, and without touching anything except the listing itself.

The "Before" Reality

Before the revamp, the quilt block listing had:

- A long, keyword-heavy title
- Photos that showed the product, but not the experience
- A description that explained the kit, but didn't steady the buyer
- Important details buried in paragraphs
- Assumptions that buyers would "figure it out"

None of this made the listing bad.

But it made it tiring.

Buyers had to:

- interpret
- imagine
- infer
- reassure themselves

And tired buyers don't buy.

The product wasn't failing.
The listing was asking too much.

What We Did Not Change

This matters as much as what we did change.

We did not:

- lower the price
- add free shipping
- change the product
- add bonuses
- run promotions
- change ads
- chase new keywords
- follow trends

The offer stayed the same.

Only the listing changed.

That's what makes this a valid test.

Applying the 5-Part Framework (In Real Life)

Here's how the listing was rebuilt — not by guessing, but by intentionally supporting buyer decisions.

PART 1: Instant Recognition

Before:
The listing relied on keywords to explain what it was.

After:
The title and hero image work together to immediately signal:

- DIY
- wood
- quilt-inspired
- easy
- customizable

A buyer doesn't need to think.

They recognize themselves or they move on.

PART 2: Safety & Reassurance

Before:
The listing assumed buyers understood the process.

After:
We directly addressed fear:

- "You can't mess this up."
- "It's just paint."
- "Paint over it if you don't like it."

We normalized hesitation instead of pretending it didn't exist.

This alone removed a major conversion blocker.

PART 3: Effort Reality Check

Before:
Time and effort were implied, not stated.

After:
We clarified:

- This is a relaxed project
- It takes a couple of hours
- It's finishable
- It fits into real life

This prevented buyers from imagining worst-case scenarios.

PART 4: Emotional Payoff

Before:
The listing focused on what the kit was.

After:
The listing focused on:

- the enjoyment of the process
- the pride of finishing
- the joy of choosing colors
- the satisfaction of display or gifting

Buyers could picture the outcome — and themselves in it.

PART 5: Decision Removal

Before:
Important questions were answered — but scattered.

After:
We gathered reassurance into clear sections:

- What's included
- What you need
- Size
- Skill level
- Shipping
- Gifting
- Natural wood variation

Nothing critical was left to chance.

Why This Matters More Than Optimization

Most Etsy advice focuses on:

- traffic
- keywords
- algorithms

This rebuild focused on:

- human hesitation
- emotional safety
- decision fatigue

And that's why it works.

When a listing removes doubt, it doesn't need tricks.

The Key Lesson

This wasn't a miracle.
It was not luck.
It was not timing.

It was alignment.

The listing finally matched:

- how buyers think
- how they browse
- how they decide

And when that happens, even an older listing can earn again.

Pause Here (One Last Time)

Before moving on:

- Look at your own chosen listing
- Ask yourself:
    - Where is my buyer doing extra mental work?
    - Where am I assuming understanding?
    - Where am I explaining instead of reassuring?

That's where your opportunity lives.

WORKBOOK PAGE — SECTION 4

Before & After Observation

Purpose:
Teach sellers how to see what changed — not guess.

Before Revision — Notes

What felt unclear or heavy in the listing before?

After Revision — Notes

What feels calmer, clearer, or easier now?

What Stayed the Same (Important)

Check all that apply:

- ☐ Product
- ☐ Price
- ☐ Shipping
- ☐ Materials
- ☐ Offer

This confirms the change was the listing, not the product.

SECTION 5

The Repeatable Workbook

How to Fix a Listing That Should Be Selling

Insight without action is just encouragement.

This section exists so the reader doesn't walk away thinking,

> *"That makes sense… but I still don't know what to do next."*

The goal here is simple:

- one listing
- one clear process
- one calm pass at a time

Not a full shop overhaul.
Not a weekend of chaos.
Just a repeatable method that works.

Step 1: Choose the Right Listing (Again — On Purpose)

You are working on **one listing only.**

It should:

- have sold before
- have interest (favorites, views, messages)
- feel like it should be earning
- make you slightly frustrated because you know it's better than its numbers

Do not start with:

- your newest idea
- your favorite idea
- the one you're emotionally attached to
- the one that has never sold

You're building confidence and proof — not testing hope.

Step 2: The Buyer Hesitation Map

Before you write anything, answer these questions honestly, without editing.

What might make someone hesitate before buying this?
(Too hard? Too expensive? Too much time? Fear of messing it up?)

What questions would they need answered to feel safe clicking "Add to Cart"?
(Size, skill level, supplies, shipping, gifting, time, returns.)

What reassurance would make this feel like a good decision — not a risky one?

This becomes the backbone of your listing.
Not your product description.
Your decision support system.

Step 3: Match Hesitations to the 5-Part Framework

Now take what you uncovered and place it where it belongs:

Recognition issues → Title & hero image

Fear or doubt → Early reassurance language

Time/effort confusion → Clear expectations

Emotional uncertainty → Process + outcome imagery

Last-minute anxiety → FAQs & clarity sections

You are no longer guessing what to fix.

You are responding to real hesitation.

Step 4: The Image Purpose Planner

Every image must earn its spot.

Before adding or changing photos, label each image with a job:

- Recognition
- Reassurance
- Process
- Scale
- What's Included
- Creative Freedom
- Instructions Peek
- Finished Result
- Trust / Proof

If an image doesn't answer a question or remove doubt, it's decoration.

Decoration doesn't convert.

Step 5: The Description Backbone (Not a Wall of Text)

Your description is not meant to be read top to bottom.

It is meant to be:

- skimmed
- jumped through
- landed on at random

Use:

- clear headers
- short paragraphs
- calm language
- repetition where it reduces anxiety (not where it bloats)

You are not teaching.
You are steadying.

Step 6: The "Leave It Alone" Rule

This is the step that makes or breaks everything.

Once you revise the listing:

- do not tweak
- do not optimize
- do not second-guess
- do not react emotionally

Give the listing time to:

- settle
- re-index
- gather behavior signals
- earn trust

Most sellers sabotage good work by never letting it breathe.

You don't need constant motion.
You need clean observation.

Step 7: Weekly Observation (Not Obsession)

Track weekly:

- views
- favorites
- orders
- conversion rate
- messages

You are watching for:

- increased confidence
- fewer confused questions
- steadier conversion
- better quality traffic

You are not chasing spikes.
You are watching direction.

Why This Works (and Keeps Working)

This system:

- does not depend on trends
- does not rely on hacks
- does not burn you out
- does not require constant reinvention

It respects:

- human behavior
- real attention spans
- decision fatigue
- your time and energy

And once you've done it once, you can do it again — calmly, intentionally, and with confidence.

Pause Here (Final Workbook Pause)

Before moving on:

- Choose your one listing
- Complete the hesitation map
- Identify which of the 5 parts is weakest
- Fix only that part

You don't need to do everything.
You just need to do the right thing.

WORKBOOK PAGE — SECTION 5

The Listing Fix Plan

Purpose:
Turn insight into one calm action.

Step 1: Buyer Hesitation Map

Biggest hesitation holding buyers back:

Step 2: Where Will I Fix It?

This hesitation will be addressed in:

- ☐ Title
- ☐ Hero Image
- ☐ Image sequence
- ☐ Description Opening
- ☐ FAQ section

(Choose only one.)

Step 3: What I Will Change (Briefly)

Step 4: What I Will NOT Touch

List at least two things you promise not to change yet:

1.

2.

SECTION 6

When NOT to Touch a Listing
(And Why Most Etsy Advice Quietly Fails)

Most sellers don't fail because they don't try hard enough.

They fail because they try to fix **everything** — all the time.

This section exists to give you boundaries.
And boundaries are what keep good listings from being ruined by panic.

The Most Common Mistake Sellers Make

Here's the pattern almost every struggling seller falls into:

- A listing doesn't sell
- Panic sets in
- Advice is consumed
- Something is changed
- Then something else
- Then something else
- Then everything

At no point does the seller stop long enough to know:

What actually worked?

This isn't optimization.
It's reaction.

And reaction kills good listings quietly.

When You Should NOT Touch a Listing

These moments are critical.
Ignore them, and you'll undo good work.

❌ Do NOT touch a listing immediately after revising it

Listings need time to:

- re-index
- re-settle in search
- collect behavioral signals
- be interpreted by buyers

Changing things too quickly resets that process.

If you revise a listing and immediately start tweaking:

- you never get clean data
- you never know what helped
- you stay stuck in guesswork

Minimum rule:
Give it at least 30 days before making conclusions.

❌ Do NOT touch a listing because "someone online said…"

This includes:

- YouTube thumbnails
- Instagram reels
- TikTok hot takes
- "Etsy gurus"
- Even Etsy's own generic tips

Advice without context is noise.

Your shop:

- has history
- has data
- has patterns
- has a specific buyer

What works for a new digital shop selling $5 printables is not the same as what works for a made-to-order, hands-on DIY kit.

Your job is not to follow advice.
Your job is to evaluate relevance.

❌ Do NOT touch a listing because sales dipped for a few days

Sales are not a straight line.

Traffic fluctuates.
Buyers pause.
Weekends differ.
Seasons matter.

Short-term dips do not equal failure.

If you react to every quiet stretch, you'll never build stability.

Watch trends — not moods.

❌ Do NOT touch a listing that is selling consistently

This sounds obvious — but it's where many sellers self-sabotage.

If a listing is:

- selling
- converting
- receiving good reviews
- being favorited

Leave it alone.

Do not "improve" it.
Do not "optimize" it.
Do not "test something new."

Selling listings don't need fixing.
They need protecting.

Why Most Etsy Advice Fails

Most advice is built on:

- averages
- generalizations
- platform-wide assumptions

It's not built on:

- your data
- your buyers
- your product
- your energy limits

That's why sellers feel like they're doing everything "right" — and still not seeing results.

They're following advice designed for someone else.

The Difference Between Strategy and Noise

Noise says:
"Change something. Anything."

Strategy says:
"Observe first. Then decide."

This guide is not about constant motion.
It's about **intentional stillness** — followed by precise action.

The Rule That Saves Everything

Before touching a listing, ask:

> *"What specific buyer hesitation am I trying to remove?"*

If you can't answer that clearly, don't touch it.

Changing things without purpose doesn't move you forward.
It keeps you busy.

The Calm Seller Advantage

Sellers who win long-term are not the busiest.
They are the calmest.

They:

- change one thing at a time
- wait for results
- trust observation
- protect what works
- stop chasing noise

This is how listings earn their keep.
And how sellers keep theirs.

Final Pause (This One Matters)

If you take nothing else from this guide, take this:

You do not need to fix everything.
You do not need to know everything.
You do not need to react to everything.

You need:

- clarity
- restraint
- and the courage to let good work breathe

That's how confidence replaces chaos.

WORKBOOK PAGE — SECTION 6

The "Leave It Alone" Commitment

Purpose:
Prevent sabotage through over-tweaking.

My Observation Window

I will observe this listing for:

- ☐ 30 days
- ☐ 60 days
- ☐ 90 days

During this time, I will NOT:

- ☐ Rewrite the title
- ☐ Swap photos
- ☐ Change pricing
- ☐ Chase new advice

What I WILL Track Weekly

- ☐ Views
- ☐ Favorites
- ☐ Orders
- ☐ Conversion rate
- ☐ Buyer questions

Reminder (Write This In Your Own Words)

> *"I don't need to fix everything.*
> *I need to let good work breathe."*

FINAL SECTION

How to Apply This Without Burning Out
(And Build a Shop That Earns Reliably)

By now, you understand something most Etsy sellers never stop to question:

You don't have a motivation problem.
You don't have a creativity problem.
You don't even have a "selling" problem.

You have a **focus problem** — and it was taught to you.

This final section exists to help you apply what you've learned without turning Etsy into another exhausting full-time job.

The Trap: Trying to Fix Everything at Once

Once sellers understand what's been going wrong, the instinct is to sprint:

- fix all listings
- redo the whole shop
- apply the framework everywhere
- finally "catch up"

This is where burnout happens.

Not because the system doesn't work — but because it's applied without restraint.

The goal is not to overhaul your shop.

The goal is to build a **small group of listings that earn consistently.**

The "Earning Core" Concept

Every successful Etsy shop — whether the seller realizes it or not — has an earning core.

These are the listings that:

- sell repeatedly
- attract the right buyers
- require less explanation
- feel easier to support
- justify their time and energy

Your job is not to make everything earn.

Your job is to identify and protect your earning core.

A Sustainable Way Forward (Step-by-Step)

Step 1: Choose One Listing at a Time

Apply this system to:

- one listing
- then wait
- then observe
- then decide

Momentum built slowly lasts longer.

Step 2: Stop Reviving What the Market Already Rejected

If a listing:

- has never sold
- gets no favorites
- receives no questions
- drains your energy

It does not deserve rescuing.

Letting go is not failure.
It's strategy.

Step 3: Duplicate What Works — Calmly

When one listing earns:

- don't immediately "improve" it
- don't overthink it
- don't disrupt it

Instead:

- note what decisions it supports well
- apply those principles to another deserving listing

You're building consistency, not chaos.

You are allowed to build a shop that works for you.

Not one that drains you.

The Real Outcome of This Guide

If you apply this system honestly, one of two things will happen:

1. Some listings will earn again
2. Some listings will reveal they never should have been fixed

Both outcomes are wins.

Because clarity beats hope.
Every time.

Final Words (From One Seller to Another)

You don't need more advice.
You don't need more strategies.
You don't need to be someone else.

You need:

- to trust what you already know
- to listen to your data
- to stop fighting the process
- and to let good work breathe

That's how listings earn their keep.

And that's how you do too.

You are allowed to build a shop that works for you.

Not one that drains you.

The Real Outcome of This Guide

If you apply this system honestly, one of two things will happen:

1. Some listings will earn again

2. Some listings will reveal they never should have been fixed

Both outcomes are wins.

Because clarity beats hope.
Every time.

Final Words (From One Seller to Another)

You don't need more advice.
You don't need more strategies.
You don't need to be someone else.

You need:

- to trust what you already know
- to listen to your data
- to stop fighting the process
- and to let good work breathe

That's how listings earn their keep.

And that's how you do too.

WORKBOOK PAGE — FINAL SECTION

Building an Earning Core

Purpose:
Help sellers think long-term without overwhelm.

My Current Earning Core

List the listings that already show promise:

1.

2.

3.

Listings I Will Stop Pouring Energy Into (For Now)

1.

2.

3.

(Letting go is not failure.)

Final Reflection

Finish this sentence:

"If I focused on fewer listings, I would feel…"

Before You Publish the Next Listing

You don't need more tricks.
You don't need to chase trends, rewrite everything overnight, or turn yourself into someone you're not.

You just need to stop building listings that ask for attention —
and start building listings that earn it.

A listing earns its keep when:

- It respects the buyer's time
- It answers the real questions before they're asked
- It removes friction instead of adding pressure
- It lets the product and experience speak clearly

If this book has done its job, you now see your listings differently.
You can feel when something is missing.
You can spot confusion before a buyer ever reaches the checkout page.

That awareness is the real shift.

You don't need to overhaul your shop all at once.
Start with one listing.
Let it earn.
Then move to the next.

Quiet progress beats frantic change every time.

Before You Hit Publish

Short, calm checklist:

Does this listing answer the buyer's first three questions without them scrolling?

Can someone understand what this is in under five seconds?

Do the images carry the information, not just the beauty?

Is the experience clear, not just the product?

Would you feel confident buying this without messaging the seller?

That's it.

No overwhelm.
No 47-step monster list.

You've created a listing that earns its keep.

Made in the USA
Monee, IL
05 November 2026

67384098R00026